Aggressive Deer Management

The Fast Track to Trophy Bucks

A Comprehensive Guide
To
Aggressive Deer Management
The Technique For Rapid Results

By

Zacch Smith

www.AggressiveDeerManagement.com

© 2003 by Zacch Smith. All rights reserved.

No part of this book may be reproduced, stored in a retrieval system, or transmitted by any means, electronic, mechanical, photocopying, recording, or otherwise, without written permission from the author.

ISBN: 1-4107-4749-2 (e-book)
ISBN: 1-4107-4750-6 (Paperback)
ISBN: 1-4107-4751-4 (Hardcover)

Library of Congress Control Number: 2003093030

This book is printed on acid free paper.

Printed in the United States of America
Bloomington, IN

1stBooks – rev. 5/30/03

Dedication

I dedicate this book to my wife Linda and my daughter Christine. They lovingly fill my life with everything I need, above and beyond my Whitetail hunting adventures.

I cherish both of you.

Zacch Smith

Aggressive Deer Management will work on your lease!

- Super aggressive management technique for the fastest possible results
- Low fence or high fence
- Large or small acreage
- Straight answers to your management questions
- Supplemental feeding
- Important cull determination information
- The management guide for every trophy hunter

Contents

Foreword xi

Philosophical And Conceptual Foundation xiii

Preliminary Thoughts xix

Muy Grand Purpose xxi

Chapters

I. Carrying Capacity 1
    A. Carrying capacity defined 3
    B. Proper carrying capacity for maximum results 7

II. Ratio Rationalization 23
    A. How to determine the present buck to doe ratio 25
    B. Census methods you can use 30
    C. How to adjust the buck to doe ratio 42

III. Implementing Your Ratio Strategy 47
    A. What is the proper buck to doe ratio 49
    B. Let's talk numbers 58

	C. When to harvest the excess does in your herd	62
	D. When to harvest the cull bucks in your herd	69
IV.	How to Ascertain A Cull Buck	75
	A. Age consideration	77
	B. Spike bucks: cull or not?	82
	C. Freak bucks: cull or not?	88
	D. 6-point bucks: cull or not?	92
	E. Are 8-pointers culls?	96
	When to cull 8-point bucks	
	F. Brow-tine deficient bucks:	101
	to cull or not to cull	
V.	Supplemental Feeding	109
	A. Protein and mineral blocks	111
	B. Food plots	118
	C. Water availability	123
VI.	Our ADM Goal	129
	A. What scores can you expect from free ranging bucks?	131
	B. What we wish to accomplish By Administering This Technique	136

VII. Salient Synopsis For Instant Field Deployment 141
    A. Quick Guide To Management 143
    B. Order of operation 149
    C. Population Age Structure 150
    D. Management Comparison 153
    E. Synopsis 157
    F. Reflections 161
    G. Blank Forms 167

Foreword

In my quest to scribe this book, I have strived to provide information for the swiftest, most accurate method for producing the best bucks possible on any given property using cutting-edge, precise directions for exactly when you should perform the actions necessary.

I have deemed this method: Aggressive Deer Management (ADM). This technique fits hunters and landowners in today's fast paced world.

None of us have time for slow moving, haphazard plans. This guide reflects my desire to provide the most streamlined path to trophies without information overload.

I have gathered the information found herein by studious field study, spending every available moment observing deer from a hunter's, as well as a student's perspective. As my extended family can quantify, they have not seen me at the usual Thanksgiving and Christmas celebrations for the last few years; but everyone knows where I am…typically in South Texas, silently observing the whitetail deer.

Philosophical And Conceptual Foundation

Everything good is built on strong foundations, from buildings, to business, to people. Of strong, I am not speaking of wealth as much as I am of will and desire, tinted with ethics, morality and honesty. As people go, we can adapt and change, we can be molded if we choose to be pliable. The desire to hunt can make a young person very pliable and in keeping with tradition shape them inwardly to reflect the values of their hunting companions and elders whom they respect. Most senior hunters possess these traits and are happy to share their time with others. I hope some of these traits are made evident in my writing.

Questions are posed and answers are offered. The answers herein are the sum of field study, coupled with private studies performed on free ranging, whitetail deer populations. I have determined that observation of free ranging herds should be the rule rather than the exception.

When drawing conclusions on whitetail management using captive deer herds, you are limited in the conclusions that you can definitively make. The captive herd is lacking in many of the naturally occurring variables found in nature. To compound this there have been erroneous studies conducted on captured deer from areas that are, and have been, over-hunted. Places where bucks of any stature are routinely harvested just because they are bucks. In areas such as these, bucks sporting four-points or better are taken early in their life cycle, and the occasional eight or ten-point never has any chance to reach maturity so the herds in areas like this are actually being <u>reverse managed</u> to produce the lowest common denominator.

Herds such as this will most certainly be groomed, or maybe I should say doomed to produce an abnormal amount of spike deer, as well as other low quality antler combinations. This is due to the fact that lowly spikes and smallish three, four and five-point bucks are the only bucks that may be passed by a hunter in hopes of taking a little bit more substantial buck. We all know of areas and hunters like these.

No study should be deemed accurate or even considered of value that is based on deer herds from these parameters unless specifically emphasized, so the outcome can be fully understood.

There are pockets of hunters that practice reverse management all over the United States. Happily, the good news is that this type of hunting is slowly disappearing due to education available through various media. The hunting articles concerning deer management in popular shooting magazines have had a tremendous positive affect as well as local newspaper articles, sporting shows and hunter-to-hunter influences as well. This trend towards management is perpetuating though the hunting community as a whole.

If you study the progression of hunter's habits you will find that they mimic society, in general, many times over. As people grow into their early adulthood they often are more inclined to take the path of least resistance, believing that anything goes, acting with little thought of future consequences. However, as men and women mature and raise families they find themselves wanting to protect their children from the very acts they championed prior to realizing that they themselves are responsible for so much more than they originally thought.

This awakening occurs in the lives of responsible intelligent people via first hand experiences. As they age, they witness the effects that an uninhibited life style has on their peers and the children of those that maintain a life lacking organization. As they become older and wiser, they see that their guidance will either be to the nourishment or the detriment of their children. This revelation leads them to be more conservative in their actions; more deliberate with the direction they lead the future generations.

This naturally occurring evolution of enlightenment is congruent with most hunters as well. Hunters eventually realize why they harvest small inadequate bucks, and the fact that each individual hunter is responsible for guiding their own herd properly. This concept catches up with most hunters sooner or later when their desires turn to harvesting something more than the average buck. This desire will cause us to step up to the plate and take responsibility for acquiring the quality desired. Growing trophy deer requires a strong foundation, one with good genetics either by nature or our direction. This foundation must include good nutrition, as well, to make it complete.

We change our actions and prior notions and trade them in on a management plan. The plan and proactive participation produce the results we seek. The trend towards trophy management is a maturing process of whitetail hunters as a whole, it started a generation ago and has been gaining acceptance every year.

To continue this momentum, our children should be taught from the beginning. Start them off managing your herd, let them harvest does and culls in their quest for a true mature trophy buck. Many times it is too expensive to purchase a spot for the kids to harvest a trophy from a lease but helping with the culling may be welcome. Make them a working part of the management of your herd so they understand what is going on and why. You err if you allow your children to kill "pretty good" bucks with potential that would normally be passed for management purposes.

When you start children off allowing them to shoot bucks, "just because", then you are sending the wrong message. This teaches that principals and rules do not apply. Instead, build a hunting foundation that will mean something to your children for the rest of their lives.

As they cull bucks with you they will learn by example, self-control, discipline, and how to hunt and manage. Just as important they will have a graduating goal for harvesting a bigger buck and that will lead them to appreciate the challenge, instead of taking for granted that they can just shoot a buck. This will later define them as the hunters they become.

Preliminary Thoughts

I stand in awe of the magnificent quarry
I endeavor to procure.
The whitetail buck, a uniquely majestic and regal obsession.

To keen senses, proud gate and staunch display of dominance.
To pursuit, surprises, and lessons learned.

To effeminate influences in my life that allow my indulgence.
I regale, in that effeminate forces usher my quarry's approach.

To starlit nights, cool breezes and campfires.
To coveys flushing, coyotes howling and silent black nights.

To outhouses, mesquite thorns, flat tires,
and rattle snakes.

To exact calculations, educated guesses and
common sense.
To science, theories and flawless awe inspiring
creation.

To faded stripes, shadowy stars,
an off cast hue of blue.
Sacrifice made, Price paid.

To briskly Waving colors, rock solid,
more vivid than ever.
Old glory.

To hunting, hunters and the hunted.
I salute you.

By: Zacch Smith

Muy Grand Purpose

This book has been written for a grand purpose, not for grand standing, nor to provide readers with funny quips or outlandish tales. I have not provided countless pages for you to muttle through on your quest for the answers that elude you.

No, this guide is designed with one purpose, to get hunters results that you can see fast. Results that you can hang over your mantle!

Aggressive deer management will work on any size hunting property. Even if you only implement the proper culling techniques and keep your population in check, you will reap huge rewards.

Results are the product of actions. The technique in this book should be implemented immediately. This book is not supposed to be between bookends collecting dust. Take charge of your trophy-hunting destiny, don't just wait for luck, you can alter the direction of the genetics now. You can improve the dynamics of your herd quickly, don't hesitate, get started as soon as possible.

Follow the directions as I outline them and start right now. You can see the full potential of your current herd much faster than you may expect and that potential will increase each year as you stay with this simple plan!

Most properties suffer from the same very common problems that are easily correctable during this hunting season! Overpopulation, for instance, or old cull deer just taking up space and food and spreading their worthless antler traits all over the herd are familiar problems that can be addressed immediately. Well, we are not going to have that anymore.

I will explain to you exactly what to do and exactly when to do it, simple and direct instruction with the reasons behind the direction. If that's not easy enough, I also summarize the steps and give you an order of operation guide so you can quickly implement the plan and refer to the condensed section so you don't have to reread the book again.

Now it is time to join me and start this plan immediately. You will see results quickly and the results will get better every year hereafter.

Now, so you ask what is the grand purpose of this book? It is so that hunters will be able to harvest the best trophy buck their herd can produce and so that all hunters around you can quickly and easily join in on this simple plan without delay and harvest the best trophy bucks their lease can produce and so on and so on. All of the deer population in your area and surrounding areas can reach their full potential on the fast track. Motivate your neighboring hunters and then get them to motivate the hunters surrounding them. Give them a copy of this book, share in the responsibility of managing the deer on surrounding leases. You can accomplish great things when you team up, because the genetic variations of the bucks on the different properties lend themselves to your direction.

You will be pleasantly surprised by how many neighboring hunters will express great relief, knowing that you are managing your deer lease, and they will be more than happy to join you, just ask.

I am sure everyone can relate to this scenario. We all agonize over what the lease next door is harvesting, we hear a shot and cringe.

Our thoughts go to the 3-year old 130-class buck that we let walk and it drives us crazy. The other hunters on the lease next door, my friend, feel the same way about you. So don't let it linger, or there will be bucks shot that should have had a chance to reach maturity. This often is the case because the hunters on the lease next door believe that you might shoot any decent buck you see. So dispel that fear right now.

I have found that the best way to fix this problem is to break the ice yourself as soon as possible, today if you can. Like magic, the worry and the tension are gone for all parties. Everyone will benefit. Let's take whitetail trophy management to the next level. Make it grow so we aren't just managing our lease or our private property, but we are managing a region. The time for talking about trophy management is over; let's get to it.

Chapter I

Carrying Capacity

I stand in awe of the magnificent quarry I endeavor to procure. The whitetail buck, a uniquely majestic and regal obsession.

Zacch Smith

Carrying Capacity Defined

In every topic of this book we are dealing with one goal in mind: to grow the best trophy whitetail bucks possible on our property. The definitions and form of management we discuss are a direct reflection of our attainable goal of maximum antler yield.

Carrying capacity as it pertains to whitetail deer is simply put: the maximum quantity of deer that can successfully live and grow to their full potential on a given property.

We are concerned with the population of whitetails as it pertains to our goal. It is for our purpose, <u>not the maximum</u> quantity of deer that may be able to survive on a given property. In fact, we do not want to be at carrying capacity, but <u>below it,</u> to insure that the herd has the best opportunity to reach its maximum potential. <u>(read – antler growth not inhibited by malnutrition).</u> Not just this year, but year to year.

With the carrying capacity in the correct range, the whitetails will likely have enough to eat year to year; thus, a deer with a good start that continues to have good forage will reach its full potential. As it matures, it will likely be a better buck when mature, than a buck that has lived through a few bad years in conditions where the competition for food was too high from overpopulation.

A buck will likely weigh less when he is underfed, and depending on the years in his growth cycle that he is deprived of adequate food, he may be of smaller stature than would be the case if he were in a herd that is managed.

Section Summary
Let's look back

Carrying capacity is the maximum quantity of deer that can be carried by the available forage and sustain a reasonably healthy existence. This is the point where deer survive but do not thrive. Competition for food plays a big role at carrying capacity and the weather is extremely significant to whether deer are malnourished or they are reasonably healthy. This is a risky place to be for developing trophy deer, we do not want our herds in this pivotal place. To reduce the risk of overpopulation and drought-induced deprivation, we must keep the deer numbers below the saturation point by a safe margin.

Proper Carrying Capacity
For Maximum Results

For proper carrying capacity conclusions to be made, they must be based on the actual field conditions as observed on the given property.

If food sources are observed to be inadequate for the current deer population, then the herd population must be adjusted to fit the forage conditions that exist or the bucks in the herd will not be able to reach their full potential.

If by careful study of the browse line and by studious observation of the impact of foraging on the whitetail's primary food sources, you find that the available foliage has been consumed excessively and little food is left on the lower portion of the plants. You will be able to see if in fact the deer are having a serious affect on the vegetation.

When you find that foliage is much more plentiful at a higher vertical elevation level on the deer's preferred food source, you have a problem.

When deer have a hard time stretching up to reach food, and little is left down lower on the plants, the young deer will suffer substantially, and eventually all deer will suffer. This is a sure sign that the population for that property is too high at this time. Considering the prevailing circumstances, the situation is not conducive to producing the results we seek.

In order to produce healthy mature trophy bucks, they must have all the food needed to grow to their full potential.

As with every aspect of deer management, the situation on any property can and does change year to year based on rainfall amounts and how hot the summers are, as well as how cold the winters are and livestock pressure. So adjust, as needed each year.

Some years it will be necessary to reduce the herd more than others; but if you follow this guideline the effect will not be so drastic. By keeping the numbers on the low side, the deer and the habitat will fare better.

There are no magic numbers for the carrying capacity of your property. However, since whitetails are so prolific, a miscalculation by a few percent will not have a detrimental long-term effect. You can always make another adjustment next year should you decide to increase or decrease your herd. The determination should be made each year according to the livestock pressure and habitat conditions that prevail.

Ok, here you are. I know you want the number, so here is the recommendation for determining the quantity of deer you should have on your property in order to be most assured that the bucks in the herd have the chance to feed properly, and reach their full potential.

After your census and observation of the condition of the habitat, you should reduce the herd by 25% of carrying capacity, with this said I will explain.

If the habitat is in great shape and you can tell little to no impact from the deer on the preferred food sources, then you may not need to do anything in the way of reducing the overall herd for carrying capacity reasons. You may already be at an acceptable population level due to earlier efforts or natural causes.

However, if the census and the consensus of you and your fellow hunters are that there are plenty of deer on the property, then you should curb the population somewhat to keep it in check before you find yourself playing catch up and wishing you had harvested 10-20% of the population before you had to witness the browse line go up and the deer quality go down.

Now if you can see obvious evidence of overpopulation then cut the herd by at least 25% and take another look at the herd, if it is still too high cut it more. While you reduce the size of your herd, also use this opportunity to do the ratio adjustments as needed.

*Aggressive Deer Management
The Fast Track to Trophy Bucks*

The herd reduction affects the deer's ability to consume the necessary nutrients to grow the racks we desire. By decreasing the deer numbers, we increase the nutrition for each remaining deer and allow the plant life to have a chance to recuperate.

Prolonged overpopulation has long-term effects on the forage as well as the health of the whitetail deer.

If the numbers are not reduced enough, then the competition for food will still be too high and you will eventually have to cut the population numbers again.

If you remove too few, then the whole herd will suffer and the mature bucks will not reach their full potential.

When you err on the side of reducing the population a little too much, then the population will get plenty to eat and the herd will be healthy and replenish rapidly. A healthy herd will produce plenty of offspring with more twins than you will find in herds that must do without proper forage.

We don't want to be excessive or go overboard on adjusting the overall population for a given property, but a few percent low in population numbers is far better for the herd than the reverse.

Since this aspect, as well as all the other aspects of deer management, are based on our best calculations as to number of deer, condition of habitat, harvest numbers, etc, the numbers you will use will not be exact but they will be more than adequate to manage your whitetail population. Don't be scared to use your numbers, jump right in and manage that herd.

To wrap this up, reduce the deer population to well below capacity to allow for unforeseeable and albeit uncontrollable factors such as your misjudgment of the herd size, inclement weather, livestock and stress related conditions. The aforementioned less than desirable conditions are more than enough reason to keep your herd at 70 to 75% capacity so that the herd will have sufficient cushion during those adverse conditions to be able to produce the healthy trophy quality bucks we desire.

Section Summary
Let's look back

Here we see that we must make decisions based on the browse line, weather, and live stock competition for the available food sources, and the current deer population, as to how many deer we should have on the property. We also will want to keep the herd population well under capacity to insure our best chances of maintaining adequate forage during rough times such as drought, winter or other stresses that may be present.

Reducing the population to about 75% of carrying capacity will improve the nutrition for all remaining deer.

If we are off on population numbers, then it is better to be a little more conservative with how many deer you allow to inhabit the property.

Having too many deer will hurt the herd much more than if you have a few less than the property can support at the nutrition level that we must have to grow trophy bucks.

Small herds with plenty of food can replenish very fast and produce big, healthy bucks at the same time.

Whereas overpopulated herds will not produce the best bucks the herd has to offer because they will not be fed well enough to reach their peak development.

Zacch Smith

Field notes

A subordinate buck submits to the dominance of an older buck in the pictures below.

A young buck enters the scene from the left, as the older buck is walking towards us to the right.

Zacch Smith

The more mature buck is now coming in closer.

Aggressive Deer Management
The Fast Track to Trophy Bucks

The immature buck feels the heat and turns away.

He now gets hasty and quickly exits stage left as the mature buck turns to face him.

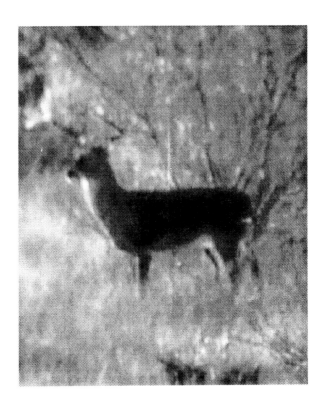

Dominance always wins out if the ratio is close enough.

Zacch Smith

Chapter II

Ratio Rationalization

To keen senses, proud

gate and staunch display

of dominance.

To pursuit, surprises

and lessons learned.

Zacch Smith

How To Determine The Present Buck To Doe Ratio

There are a few methods that can be used to determine your buck to doe ratio, as well as your overall deer numbers in general. These methods will also be used to determine the age structure of your herd. The age structure as it pertains to ADM is referring to how many deer in each age class you have. You will probably have very few mature bucks in your herd before you start managing it. You will use management to control the overall numbers as well as the age class numbers so that your herd will have 25 to 30% of its buck population in the mature age class of deer.

The easy way out is to pay someone to do a helicopter survey and if it is done at the right time of the year under the correct circumstances, then it can be the most accurate method of survey. But it will not be perfect, some deer will be counted more than once and some deer will not be seen at all.

All numbers taken by helicopters are not equal. Some pilots know the ropes from experience and some don't have a clue. Even when you know what to do, the deer don't always cooperate after they have been counted by this method a few times. Some of them learn to hold tight in cover and not run, and still others are counted two or three times, so that's why we deal with approximate best guess numbers.

Here are some methods that are used to take deer census and they work just fine.

You may want to use a couple of methods and then average the count out to obtain a closer number.

Whichever way you choose to take your survey can work, because you not only use the survey, but use your head and your knowledge of the property you are on as you manage and hunt it.

Section Summary
Let's look back

The job of determining the overall population number for the herd on your property is not a monumental task, so don't let it intimidate you.

No census numbers are perfect so your numbers will likely be as close as anyone else's numbers. The methods you can use are pretty simple and can be accomplished by anyone. You will want to take two or three census estimates and average the numbers out for guidelines.

Read on and lets get going.

*Aggressive Deer Management
The Fast Track to Trophy Bucks*

Field notes.

Zacch Smith

Census Methods You Can Use

Set up at stands spaced out to cover most of your property well inside your fence lines and spaced evenly across your property. Then set people to watch each one at the same time and use radios to take a count of every spot at the same time so no two deer will be counted twice. If you are spaced 400 yards apart and take this count thirty minutes after daybreak and 30 minutes before sundown during dark moon nights for a few days and then average the count out over the course of the census, you should have numbers close enough to work with for an age and sex break down.

Other methods include the line count and the spot light count. The line count is performed by an individual walking in a line or a path, counting the deer as he slowly moves along. You must determine the square acres that will be observed by taking that route.

Quiet vehicles can also be used when you can be seated high enough. The deer will usually exit your view shortly after they spot you, but with a high vantage point they will not usually escape being counted.

Quietly walking the line you have mapped out will usually get you close enough to count the deer on your path. By the time they spot you, depending on the level of brush, the wind direction and the terrain, you should be able to spot them.

The spotlight count and the line count are very similar but with the obvious nighttime occurrence of the spotlight count. The method you use will depend on your best judgment as to what will work best in the particular circumstances that your land requires.

The spotlight count is very effective for overall numbers and is pretty good for determining the buck to doe ratio and age classes if conducted at the right time.

The count should be taken after the bucks have hard antlers and usually a good time for this is just before the season starts. The bucks are much more outgoing when they are out of velvet and so you have a better chance of seeing them. So conducting the census in late fall is a good idea. Most bucks will be out of velvet or at least ready to shed it. By this time you will have the best chance of identifying whether a deer is a buck or a doe by the antlers. Any later than this and you may be too near the rut, depending on where you hunt and this would show skewed numbers reflecting the unusual patterns of the rut induced movement.

Usually a spotlight census is accomplished by using two spotters, a person designated to write down the numbers as called out by the spotters and a driver.

This can also be accomplished by just one person or by two working together, but for the best results get a few friends to help.

The vehicle used can vary depending on availability, topography and visibility. A truck with a safe area to perch up as high as is convenient, will work great in many cases, or just sitting on a tool box in the back of a truck may be the ticket for you.

You will start at one end of your property and drive a predetermined route from one end of the property to the other. You should try to cover all of the diverse terrain on your property, as it may exist, don't just drive the oat field you may have and calculate from that.

To get good numbers you must observe the deer across the differing range conditions that exist on your lease. You will need to determine how much property you will be viewing as you drive your route. You should determine the length of the route and multiply that by the width of the area you can effectively see deer. On any given route the width of the lane you can identify deer in will change due to the variations in vegetation and terrain so you should travel the path and record the actual approximate acreage you are viewing.

To get started take advantage of technology and use a range finder to measure an actual quantity of land that you will be observing. Start by setting up where you will start your census and write down the approximate distance that you can clearly observe from your position in both the left and right side of the trail/road that you will be driving on.

I have included this aerial to illustrate the differing view one will have on any given property. This does not pose a problem, just use your range finder and calculator to know how much land you are observing during the census.

Refer to the diagram for an example.

In this aerial photo you can see the differing terrain and the limits placed on visibility.

You must first determine the length of the trail you will follow. This can be accomplished with the odometer in your vehicle.

Next you will need to determine incrementally how far from the trail you can effectively count deer. If for example you can range 300 yards to the right and 75 yards to the left of your path then you can multiply that by the length of road by which you can see at that visibility level and come up with the square acres that have been observed.

By checking and recording the visibility range over the course of your census route, you can determine an approximate total acreage that you will be observing.

After this number is reached you may then start taking your census, and the number of deer you count can be used to come up with approximately how many deer you have per acre of land. Once the number per acre is discerned, you can multiply that by your total acreage and have a number approximating the total number of deer residing on your property.

After you have taken the census and have a number signifying the quantity of deer you believe are on your property, you divide the number of acres you have by the number of deer you counted. This will be the number you multiply by the total number of acres you are leasing, managing, or hunting.

For example, you find that on your 640-acre tract you can drive a three-mile course through the property and clearly see 200 yards along the whole way, 100 yards on each side of the trail. By this we know that 3 miles multiplied by 5,280' will equal total linear feet traveled:

3 X 5,280' = 15,840'

Now multiply that by the width of the clearly observable area which is 200 yards as measured by the range finder 200 X 3' = 600'.

Now multiply the length of the route by the width: 600' X 15,840' = 9,504,000' this is the total square footage of the area observed.

We now convert this to acres. An acre is 43,560 square feet so 9,504,000 square feet divided by 43,560 square feet is equal to 218+ acres.

If you counted 22 deer with 7 being bucks 9 being does and 6 being yearlings and fawns, then you split the young undetermined deer equally 50% bucks and 50% does so your total is 10 bucks and 12 does on the 218 acres observed.

Now we adjust that figure with the actual number of acres we hunt or manage. We will use 640 acres for example.

This equation would look like this: 640 total acres divide by 218 observed acres = 2.935. Now use this factor to access the approximate total number of deer on the property. Thus, 22 deer multiplied by the factor of 2.935=64 deer that exist on the property.

This same scenario should take place multiple times and the average of all the census counts taken should be used for the number you go by.

The census must be made during optimal times and optimal conditions to be effective.

If the deer are bedded down due to weather, wind or lunar changes then you should note that and avoid the census at those times. Deer that are bedded down are hard to spot and may not be in view at all.

Section Summary
Let's look back

Another step to management is the census. They can be taken in differing ways and with different equipment. We talked about four ways to gather information to use in your census.

You can use the previous methods to determine deer numbers as well as ratio and age breakdowns for your herd. The numbers will be workable but no number is exact on a free ranging herd in normal cover. So don't let the details slow you down, do the best you can to keep your herd in check. You can make additional adjustments to the herd if needed during the season.

If you live and breath deer and spend lots of time on your hunting property, then you may very well know exactly how your herd is doing and you may know how the population should be adjusted just by your intimate knowledge of the herd and property you hunt.

So, however you choose to decide the population control numbers can work to the advantage of the herd.

Keep the number of deer well below capacity while reducing the overall herd. Also, adjust the ratio and eliminate the cull bucks.

Aggressive Deer Management
The Fast Track to Trophy Bucks

Field notes

Zacch Smith

How To Adjust The Buck To Doe Ratio

In order to adjust the buck to doe ratio in your herd, we must take one step back and evaluate the overall range conditions and deer holding capacity of the given property.

If for example the fawn crop was small and the conditions have been too dry or you are on property with competing livestock that has depleted the food source, then this should influence your conclusion on the overall number of deer that can live successfully on the property and still have an adequate food supply to be healthy.

When the given range conditions of your herd is healthy and over-browsing is not evident, then slight preemptive population control measures may or may not be needed. In this case, an adjustment in the ratio may be all that is warranted. However, if the conditions of the habitat and the health of the deer population are at odds, then you must cut the overall number of deer on the property.

Too many deer will be detrimental to the herd and can lead to die off from starvation and disease. If you determine that the range is not sufficient, then lower the overall deer numbers while correcting the buck to doe ratio, concentrating on eliminating the poorest specimens of bucks and the oldest does. If you err, then err in the way of cutting the herd a little more than needed. The herd will benefit tremendously and the numbers by natural order will increase quickly due to the plentiful forage available to the remaining deer.

Albeit annual rainfall, particularly spring rainfall, will have huge implications to your deer management program so you should take this into consideration and adjust accordingly. On really good years stick to your plan, but on extra dry years you may need to adjust and remove more deer so that their range will be adequate to feed the deer population.

Section Summary
Let's look back

The poorest specimens of deer in the herd should be the deer that are picked for removal, along with any other older deer that may be necessary to set the numbers right. To adjust the age class of your herd you will also be required to harvest some young deer. Therefore, it is essential that you study the younger deer that must be removed and be sure to remove the deer with the least evident potential as compared to their peers.

Field notes

Zacch Smith

Chapter III

Implementing Your Ratio Strategy

To effeminate influences
in my life that allow my
indulgence.
I regale, in that
effeminate forces usher
my quarry's approach.

Zacch Smith

What Is The Proper Buck To Doe Ratio

The buck to doe ratio as it pertains to our subject is simply the number of bucks verses the number of does on a given property.

Adjusting the buck to doe ratio is a necessary part in the overall management of your deer herd. If the balance is heavy on either side, the desired result of growing quality bucks consistently is greatly reduced.

If the number of deer on a given property is too low due to predation and past hunting pressure, then eliminating does would not be in your game plan at first. However, eliminating the old bucks and especially inferior old bucks will still be necessary, as well as instantly removing any other cull bucks as they are discovered.

An old inferior buck should be harvested so that young healthy new breeding stock may take his place. Even the amount of feed consumed by the inferior buck will make a difference towards our goal.

Old bucks with undesirable antlers must be harvested or they will breed many does and perpetuate their undesirable traits to more of the deer population, who will then, in proportion to their breeding, continue to spread the inferior qualities.

When the population numbers are low, this sometimes presents a great chance to start off right. With the elimination of any inferior deer early on, before the number of deer reach our desired capacity level for the given property, the stage is set for great rewards.

There are erroneous beliefs out there that say you should not cull any buck until he is mature, but that is illogical. These misguided beliefs result in: unnecessary forage consumption, undue stress related to competition and occasionally a cull that goes nocturnal and is able to perpetuate his undesirable traits.

If this is not enough reason, then consider that it will be impossible to keep the ratio at the desired level, without harvesting some bucks in the younger age classes of deer. In most every scenario, in order to keep the ratio in check and the overall population at the desired capacity level, you must eliminate bucks as well as does. There will not be enough mature bucks in the herd to harvest only mature deer, without completely eliminating that age class.

When the herd is at the proper capacity level you must harvest a number of deer that is equal to the number that is born and survives each year in order to maintain the level. If you harvest less than that number, your herd will grow and exceed the capacity level desired.

Although we should not cull baby bucks unless the fawn crop is so great that it becomes necessary, we should cull any 2, 3, 4, 5, or 6-year old buck that is obviously a cull. Anything less will be to the detriment of the herd. During culling each year we are keeping the best that the herd has to offer and eliminating the poorest specimens.

When you determine the number of bucks that you must remove, you will be removing the two-year old and older spike's, 3-pointers, 4-pointers and 5-pointers. The bucks in any age group that shows far less potential than the other average bucks in the age group should be culled. As the cull gets to maturity, he may be more elusive and survive to breed in his old age. Don't let that happen!

When a herd must be developed and you actually need more deer in the herd, you should eliminate all undesirable bucks immediately so your best bucks will be the only ones with a chance to breed. When you have a low number of bucks, each buck will be a huge percentage of the genetic pool of offspring, so the buck allowed to breed should only be the best your herd has to offer.

When the deer numbers you have to start off with are low, the herd benefits from lack of pressure for food as it populates the herd with fawns. These new additions to the herd are deer bred from the bucks you choose to leave in the group, which should be the best examples of the deer on that property.

If the number of bucks are higher than the number of does, then the bucks will suffer undue stress during the rut that will lead to much higher mortality rates.

The competition for the does can increase to dangerous levels that are detrimental to the bucks. The burden would be enormous and the excessive fighting would lead to major injuries and death.

The increased stress level of the bucks will contribute to the buck's overall health decline at the worst possible time, during and after the rut. A buck enduring stress for long periods of time, suffers physically not unlike we do.

In trying times, as you well know, even people are said to have become ill from being overly stressed. Well there is a reason for this.

In the case of the buck, his metabolic rate increases in times of stress, which in turn burns up whatever energy he has stored in the form of fat. He uses up much more of his energy when the ratio is skewed then would be necessary if the ratio is correct. Many times the buck will not be able to completely recover in time to grow his antlers to his full potential.

However, when we turn the table and have too many does, the competition is low and this leads to unwanted results. The unnecessary does help to deplete the food sources and this in turn leaves the bucks with less forage producing smaller antlers.

When the doe numbers are out of hand, the older mature desirable bucks are not able to keep up with the many does that are ready to be bred. So less desirable younger bucks, which may not have been old enough for a good determination as to its worthiness, are able to breed does. Thus, a cull buck not having yet been culled or even determined to be a cull, can breed does if the doe numbers are not maintained. This being the case, you have little power over steering the genetic composition of the herd.

Section Summary
Let's look back

The buck to doe ratio must be kept in check for optimal results. Correct ratio balance contributes to the overall health of the herd. It lessens stress and greatly improves the chances of your plan to allow only good mature bucks to breed, thus enhancing the genetic pool.

Cull bucks should be removed! No determined cull should ever be allowed to remain in the herd. The key here is accurately determining which bucks to cull! (Refer to chapters on determining cull bucks).

Keeping the doe numbers in check removes the opportunity of younger bucks to breed does, this being very important as the younger bucks may later be deemed culls.

We have gone over the range of consideration you should look at to decide the number of deer that should be removed. The outcome will depend on weather, current numbers and livestock competition. The ratio percentage number is discussed in the Let's Talk Numbers chapter to follow. Even though the ratio should remain a constant, the population will vary depending on field conditions.

Field notes

Let's Talk Numbers

In the quest for the right answer to the question of what is the right ratio, one answer is evident based on what the ratio must accomplish in its role as our deer management tool.

Controlling the ratio gives us the ability to control the breeding, and by controlling the breeding through the herd ratio and the culling of inferior undesirable bucks, we are then able to direct the genetics of the herd immediately. Altering the traits we do not want and encouraging the antler dynamics we do want.

The ratio of bucks to does in a herd managed for antler quality (trophy bucks) should be no more than 1 to 1.25 does per 1 buck.

Logic behind the statement.

With this accomplished, the forage will be more equally shared by both the bucks and the does; thus allowing the bucks to forage on nutritious vegetation usually consumed by does and fawns.

The dominate bucks will breed the does. As anyone who has spent considerable time observing deer habits will tell you subordinate bucks submit and avoid confrontation over hot does, the dominant bucks <u>will</u> breed the does.

When the numbers are in check there are enough mature bucks to take care of the does as they cycle in. Keeping this plan in balance insures that next year this cycle continues. The young bucks will not be able to breed a doe because of the competition from older bucks, thus avoiding having a buck breed that may later be deemed a cull.

Section Summary
Let's look back

The buck to doe ratio should be 1 to 1.25 does to 1 buck for optimal results. This promotes control of the genetic direction though culling the inferior bucks coupled with low doe numbers. As a result you will experience better bucks and less culls showing up in the mix.

Aggressive Deer Management
The Fast Track to Trophy Bucks

Field notes

Zacch Smith

When To Harvest The Excess Does In Your Herd

This is another area in the overall deer management equation that justifies discussion.

Aggressive Deer Management (ADM) is the method we are using and I believe that the same answer that applies to this plan also should apply universally to management plans in general.

Some would have you believe that does should be harvested at the end of the season, and most hunters harvest them at that time. Some say that it doesn't matter when you harvest them and I guess if you have plenty of years to slowly see results, then maybe you can use other methods of management. But as for me I know I have far too few hunting seasons left. Unfortunately we only get to hunt as our schedule allows, and since the season only comes once a year most of us realize our own mortality and don't wish to waste any more time than necessary to tag trophy bucks. So that is where this all ties together.

Let's examine my reasoning for the answer. Conventional wisdom tells you to harvest them at the end of the season. However, this is not logical. By this time, they are through the biggest part of winter in many areas and most vegetation no matter where you hunt is usually dormant (dead, brown, not growing) and has been for some time. Many times an early cold spell shuts off the food supply prematurely and that leaves the herd with much less food for the high stress rut period and the normally tough time of winter. Should the herd have to share its diminishing food supply with deer you intend to cull anyway?

In addition to this, the bucks are now competing for food with deer that you intend to remove. They also have to deal with the added exhaustion of chasing and breeding more does. You should know that this situation augments the problem of unacceptable bucks having a much easier time of finding a receptive doe, while the breeder buck is occupied with another.

Now to add to this, at the end of the season you are finally ready to harvest the excess does, and guess what? Now they are all bred, so after one of your best bucks has eventually been able to breed his share of does, you now, by harvesting a doe that needs to be removed for population control are also harvesting his offspring. This is not a logical way to manage.

This poses a more important problem then you may realize. Can you tell which doe's have been bred by a mature breeder that you left in the herd, and which one was bred by the cull that got lucky because the better buck was occupied with another hot doe because the ratio was adjusted too late?

In essence, to take your does late is a disservice to your herd in general, and especially to your achievable goal of growing trophy class deer.

With that said lets enact Aggressive Deer Management. <u>Harvest the excess does as soon as you legally can</u>. Don't allow them to consume one bite of nutrients needed for your herd, don't allow them to be chased and bred.

Aggressive Deer Management
The Fast Track to Trophy Bucks

Aggressive Deer Management is just that. It gives every available nutrient to the most valuable deer, by aggressively taking control. It helps to eliminate the all too real chance of lesser bucks having an opportunity to breed by keeping the ratio in check before breeding takes place.

Another benefit that comes from this technique is that the forage not consumed by the does that are harvested at the correct time will be available for all of the remaining deer during the time that it is most needed, the breeding season; and as we know, this coincides with the winter months, when the nutrient value of food is low and the quantity is even lower.

Be creative when harvesting the excess does, you can remove them at locations other than your favorite hunting spot. They can be harvested on your way back to camp or at alternate preset locations chosen so as not to interfere with your primary hunting spots. You may elect to have a guest hunt for the does in these predetermined locations.

There are many scenarios that can be used so pick the one that works for you.

Section Summary
Let's look back

One of the important structures of aggressive deer management is when to harvest the excess does in the herd. The reasons are discussed in this chapter and it is made clear that you should harvest the does at the earliest possible time. If you take advantage of bow season dispatch them then, or if not, then do it on opening weekend.

Zacch Smith

Field notes

When To Harvest The Cull Bucks In Your Herd

ADM will work on any deer herd if implemented and maintained. The tenets of ADM all work with one another and help to justify each other, just as the reasons behind the timing of the doe reductions show their merit by explanation of what can happen if you don't follow the plan.

This topic, as in every other topic, goes hand in hand with the other subjects as they relate to the whole concept of ADM. The complications previously mentioned regarding the removal of does late in the season can be amplified greatly by late removal of cull bucks. This really makes a mess of a management program.

By harvesting them late in the season you promote inadequate bucks breeding does that should have been removed. You have inferior antlered bucks competing and in many cases winning the does because of age and dominance and you have the very real possibility of culls injuring your best stock fighting over hot does. So in a very real scenario you may then lose a good buck due to being injured by a cull. When you do finally get around to taking your culls, they have already consumed much of the precious winter forage and the does you harvest late may be from your good stock leaving the culls offspring to steer your genetic pool.

So what do you think the answer is regarding when to harvest the cull bucks in your herd? I am sure that through deductive reasoning you are way ahead of me by now, and you are right. On opening day, its hammer time, make sure you are making the right call and get those culls outta there. (Refer to determining a cull.)

Don't let the cull bucks walk because you don't want to spook the huge trophy buck you are imagining may be about to walk out of the brush. Our goal is to have many trophy bucks. So manage your property and get rid of the cull while you still see him, so future generations of bucks standing in front of you will not show that inferior genetic trait you don't want.

If you let him walk you will probably see more inferior bucks just like him for years to come so you must alter the course of the genetic line right now ASAP. Just shoot 'em already! The other deer may not even run off. You know the drill, you've seen it before, most of the time they come right back or even just stand there and continue to eat. So there is no excuse. Have you pulled the trigger yet?

Now, every deer with a small set of antlers or other apparent defect is not a cull buck, so make sure you read the section on determining a cull before you implement this part of the ADM plan.

Section Summary
Let's look back

Again here we have discussed the reasons behind the answer and this too is an important part of Aggressive Deer Management. <u>Cull bucks should be eliminated as soon as they are determined a cull. Don't let them take one step after you have determined that they need to be removed</u>. Cull bucks should be culled throughout the entire season as they are identified. The earlier they are removed, the better it is for the herd.

*Aggressive Deer Management
The Fast Track to Trophy Bucks*

Field notes

Zacch Smith

Chapter IV

How to Ascertain a Cull Buck

To starlit nights, cool breezes and camp fires. To coveys flushing, coyotes howling, and silent black nights.

Zacch Smith

Age Consideration

ADM school of thought is now in session.

Age is the most important factor followed by range conditions and evident antler potential. A whitetail buck cannot be determined a cull when he is still a baby.

Age is tricky and plays such an important role in antler growth especially during the earliest stages of a buck's life. Later as a buck matures and he finally has a chance to show what he has or doesn't have, the subtle difference in age will become less evident.

Deer are bred during the rut. The rut starts very early for some does and much later for many others. There are does that are bred unbelievably late as I have witnessed fawns with spots that can barely get around just before season opening in Texas.

The rut definitely has a peak time when most of the chasing is witnessed, but its not 100% over just because you don't see continual chasing. After the rut peak there will be days when there are no does in the area in a receptive condition and the rut is much less evident.

Does can and do come into heat at differing times often attributable to when they themselves were born. If they were born late, then they may barely be reaching that maturity level and cycle later than does born earlier. This usually occurs only in the young doe's first cycle. If they did not become impregnated on the first go round they may cycle again approximately 30 days later.

So what I have been leading up to is that young bucks running together may appear to be different ages when actually they where born in the same year; however, months apart. That is equal to a very large percentage of a young bucks life and sets him up so he can not take advantage of the warmer months bounty, but instead is forced to deal with winters rough effects on his food supply. A couple of months will make a huge difference in the size of a yearling. Being born later in the year compromises his health and nutrition, and that directly affects his antler growth. This effect will linger, as the bucks born at the earliest possible times will have an overall size and antler development advantage until they reach maturity. The significance of the difference is much more noticeable in the young bucks.

The next most important factor is the habitat conditions. Bucks can't grow their best antlers in a drought with little available food. In the following chapters, I address most scenarios concerning culls so antler potential and cull determination is next. While reading the following chapters keep this one in mind because age does make a difference.

Section Summary
Let's look back

Age is discussed here as it pertains to the size of a deer as well as the way it pertains to our perceived guess at how old a deer is.

Age is relative to size and antler growth and the judgment of potential. This is also a major point to consider when assessing a buck for cull status.

Field notes

Zacch Smith

Spike Bucks: Cull Or Not?

A lot of debate and numerous studies have been done to conclude the answer to this question. However, some of the studies have been flawed so their answers are useless. A high fence study on a contaminated gene pool with the propensity to grow spike antlers is not the way to evaluate this subject.

The answers to managers and hunters questions must come from free ranging herds just like we typically hunt. I am aware of a private study that backs my conclusions up completely. In the private study with tagged free ranging spike bucks, the study turned out like this. Some of the deer were never seen again after the first year, but of the ones that returned year after year (60% returned) <u>all</u> grew respectable antlers. Some were average and a couple made the 150 class. These deer were studied in South Texas on a normal healthy free ranging herd with naturally occurring genetic variances. This property is managed and protein is provided with feeders just as anyone can do.

Here is the answer, ADM to the rescue.

As stated in the previous chapter don't cull baby bucks, you have no idea what they may become and a yearling spike is no indication of anything. Bucks born very late will often have only nubs or spikes and yearling bucks that were born late will be very similar. But these same deer can turn out to be impressive trophies if allowed to reach an age that will more determine actual antler potential.

When a buck reaches two years of age and has had great habitat and you note that every other two year old buck you see is an eight or ten point buck, then the likelihood that the spike two year old has genetic traits that are undesirable does exist and he should go.

However, if you are unsure of his age and you are keeping your ratio pretty well in hand, then he has no chance of breeding, being as he is inexperienced and a subordinate buck. You have plenty of time to evaluate him again next year if you wish.

A two-year old buck will be much larger than a fawn or yearling and should be distinguishable. If due to population control you need to remove bucks, then by all means pick the one with the least potential if you are confident of his age.

In the event you have a really bad drought and poor food conditions, then you can expect to see more spikes. In this scenario, adjust your thinking to the fact that a deer cannot produce normal antler growth if he is malnourished. Let them grow a bit so you can make an informed decision.

Don't eliminate your up coming crop because they were underfed during bad times.

Common since is very important to game management. If you are inundated with spike bucks, then you will be able to determine, based on your habitat conditions and the age of the spikes, if you have a genetic emergency and need to eliminate several spike bucks. In most herds they are uncommon, the exception, rather than the rule. You will find that most two-year old spikes should be eliminated and any three-year old or older spike should be eliminated from the herd without a second thought about it. Don't let him walk; take him out of the mix now, no matter what the range conditions.

Section Summary
Let's look back

In this chapter we looked at spike bucks and what makes a spike a spike. We looked at the relation of age and nutrition as well as genetics to determine if a spike should be culled.

There are spikes that should not be harvested as well as spikes that should be harvested immediately.

Aggressive Deer Management
The Fast Track to Trophy Bucks

Field notes

Zacch Smith

Freak Bucks: Cull Or Not?

I don't hear a lot about this subject, although I must say it has been around the campfire a time or two; the logic for determination that should be used is simple.

Some freak bucks are tremendous non-typical trophies. If the antlers he sprouts will make an interesting trophy, then he may be left to grow, depending on your assessment of his traits and his age.

Aggressive Deer Management
The Fast Track to Trophy Bucks

If he is a mature 5 or 6-year old buck, he will be either a trophy or not. Take him out of the herd either way, you'll hang him on the wall or keep him from breeding, don't take a chance at this age. If the odd antlers look to be caused by an injury and he is young, then look at him again next year.

In most all cases young freaks should be given a chance to blossom into a non-typical trophy, or be culled before reaching maturity, and breeding stature. Judge them relative to their antler growth potential biased by age and nothing else.

Section Summary
Let's look back

Freak bucks: sometimes they are freak culls and sometimes they are magnificent non-typical trophies. Just follow the advice and make your decision.

Aggressive Deer Management
The Fast Track to Trophy Bucks

Field notes

Zacch Smith

Six-Point Bucks: Cull Or Not?

Six-point bucks are common in most herds as young deer, especially in drought years. With all things being equal they still are not equal. Even though there may be adequate forage available, there is no guarantee that each individual buck will at a young age choose the best most appropriate forage for himself. As he matures and broadens his range, he is more likely to fill his nutritional needs more efficiently.

Young deer (yearlings to 2-year olds) that are six-point bucks should be allowed to grow a while longer, unless you need to remove some bucks for population or ratio control. Then if the six-pointer is a lesser deer than his peers, take him out of the herd.

Three-year olds are still young but that is where you should draw the line. If he is three years old and is a mere six-point buck with no noticeable potential, don't let him take up space in your herd.

The only exceptions are if the six-point is huge, super wide or fantastic by some other description, then you on your own desire to take him as a trophy, may let him mature. The other reason would be due to a severe drought condition that you know had a big impact on your herd resulting in a few six-point bucks when you do not usually produce that many.

Basically, as you manage your herd, six-point bucks that are three-years old will be very rare and the point count in the overall buck population will average higher as time progresses.

So use your best judgment when assessing bucks to be culled. Take into account all that makes him what he is. By comparing him to others in his age class you can better judge him. Do not allow age to slip out of the equation. If the six-point buck is young and small in stature and is the product of a drought, then he may very well be impressive as a 5 or 6-year old buck during better range conditions.

Section Summary
Let's look back

To determine a cull is pretty easy with a six-point buck. There are a few parameters that will guide you, such as age, habitat conditions and an actual comparison of him with the other deer in his age class. There will be six-point bucks that should walk, for example, when the deer is very young or when he is relatively young and coming out of a drought year. Typically older sixes should be harvested as soon as they are spotted.

Aggressive Deer Management
The Fast Track to Trophy Bucks

Field notes

Zacch Smith

Are 8-Pointers Culls?
When To Cull 8-Point bucks

Once an eight, always an eight?

Well, I know many people believe this, and understandably so. The deer herds they are observing may have a high concentration of eight-point bucks and little or no genetic make up for ten-points or better. So many times they do definitely remain eight-point bucks throughout their life.

This is often the situation on property that is not managed for trophy deer. Every time a ten-point walks out he is harvested. In so doing the hunters are dooming themselves, or the hunters that follow them, to genetically challenged deer herds. These herds have been directed in the path they follow by shallow, greedy consumption of the young ten-point or better bucks as they emerge, until eventually the genes that produce that trait are buried pretty deep in the gene pool.

Do eight-pointers always remain eight-point bucks? Absolutely not, when a buck reaches maturity and no longer needs so much of his nutritional resources for growing his skeletal system, a wonderful occurrence takes place. The nutrients once used to expand his skeletal structure now go to grow his antlers. Anything goes at this point, whatever genetics he may posses will be made evident.

On good years bucks can increase their antler size tremendously, they add points, kickers, main beam length, mass, width, and all the traits we desire. They are limited only by their genetic code and our ability to steer it.

A good percentage of bucks will add points during their 5th and 6th year and beyond. They can add main beam points as well as abnormal or kicker points, which add tremendous attributes to the character of a buck.

I have witnessed eight-point bucks grow to ten-point bucks, as well as ten-point bucks grow to eleven and twelve-points (and also the reverse, more on that later.)

There are times when an eight-point buck is a cull. When your herd has produced a strong batch of three and four-year old bucks and you have an obviously inferior, spindly, short-tined, narrow, basket buck that is the same age as the others but grossly inferior, then use your own good judgment and harvest the inferior bucks. Those bucks are undesirable for breeders. Bucks that are not desirable are cull bucks and should be removed.

Section Summary
Let's look back

Eight-point bucks as well as the other deer discussed, have instances where they should be culled as well as when they should walk. Any older, mature buck that is an eight should be culled, and as the herd is managed over the years you may get to a point where an eight-point that is four-years old is a cull.

You will likely reach a point where you improve genetics enough that your herd produces sufficient numbers of ten-point and better bucks and you will need to be more strict on culling bucks and not allow eight-point bucks to get too close to reaching maturity. Even though some of the eights would become tens, you may have a large percentage of three-year old tens and better. If you have a herd that is really producing better bucks, then any lesser buck becomes cull material.

Zacch Smith

Field notes

Brow-Tine Deficient Bucks:
To Cull or Not to Cull

To my knowledge this subject has not been properly addressed, or at least I have not heard of information pertaining to this phenomenon, even though it is a very common question deserving an answer.

This topic is another in a long line of topics that spend a lot of time being debated around a fire, and I am sure discussed in depth for miles and miles as we travel to our hunting haunts.

Here is the answer: yes and no.

This is not a cop out, there are two answers to the question at hand. As in all phases of your management program, you and your hunting partners must use common since to derive the correct answer, as the circumstances dictate.

The reason there are two answers to this question is that the factors that determine whether or not a brow-tine deficient buck is a cull, involve as earlier, age and habitat, both being equally important. Young deer must be given the chance to let us determine their trophy potential, and we cannot do that on an average one or two-year old deer. There are exceptions to this. Some two-year old deer show amazing potential, as we have all seen in advertisements for breeding ranches.

Now let's get back on subject in the real world. There is no reason to harvest the immature bucks, they won't breed and they may impress you next year. As for three-year olds and up you must take the habitat into serious consideration as well as the strength of the brow-tines overall in your herd. Some areas produce long brow-tines, some short brow-tines and many have a mixture that is varied.

Here are my observations and recommendations. High scoring bucks many times have less than you would hope for in the way of brow-tines, as these tines are usually shorter than the rest of the tines on the majority of bucks. With this stated we move on. The health of the herd is the determining factor on the older bucks. When you have a great year nutritionally for the deer and they are all healthy then you should be very critical if you see a buck of three-years old and older without his brow-tines, harvest him immediately. Get him out of the herd; he is a cull buck.

During drought years with low food sources and malnourished deer, the answer can change. I observed more bucks without brow-tines than usual after a rough year and know that there have been ten-point bucks that only produce eight-points after going though very hard times. The brow-tines, which are usually only 1.5"– 3" long in this area, didn't grow enough to be visible; the mass was less and the other tines were shorter. So if you know the herd suffered all year, then that is a major factor in bucks not producing their brow-tines. Some of the more domineering deer may get sufficient nutrition to put decent antler growth on and some may not. So knowing your herd will help you with the answer in your situation. If you know the conditions were disastrous to the antler development, then take that into consideration.

However, if range condition were normal to good, eliminate the 3-year old and up deer without brow-tines.

Another twist you should consider is if you have really good brow-tine length in your herd, you will want to cull lesser bucks that can't produce the better brow-tines.

Now when cutting the buck population and adjusting the age class you can use a buck's lack of brow-tines in the younger age class as the reason to cull him.

Section Summary
Let's look back

In most all cases, you will need to remove three-year old or older bucks that do not produce brow-tines. Only in severe cases of drought should you consider allowing any of them to survive. If the brow tines produced by the deer in your herd are normally pretty short, then a really bad year can cause some bucks not to produce antlers as good as their previous set. You can make a judgment call on that especially if you know the buck from a previous year.

Consider now the two-year old class. If the herd is in great shape and you find that one of the two-year olds was unable to produce any brow-tines, but the rest of them produced great little sets of antlers, then cull the lesser bucks. Be careful here, as you may be disappointed when you get him up close after culling him and see that he has knots trying to protrude at the brow-tine and G-4 position, but you thought you couldn't wait to cull him later. Culling

Zacch Smith

young bucks should be avoided except for the most obvious cases.

Field notes

Zacch Smith

Chapter V

Supplemental Feeding

To outhouses, mesquite thorns, flat tires and rattlesnakes.

Zacch Smith

Protein And Mineral Blocks

Here is where we can help nature along tremendously. Protein pellets and mineral blocks are recommended for the best results. Although you will see results whether or not you use them, protein feed is an easy addition to ADM.

There are many types of protein products on the market, ranging from numerous bagged pellets to sweet block mixtures. Minerals typically come in block form, but I have also seen the powder form you apply to corn or other feeds. The molasses protein cubes are an attractant and will be devoured by varmints especially raccoons. I have observed that deer are best served when they are fed the pellet form of protein.

I have also found that deer dislike some brands and will refuse to eat it at all, but when substituted with another brand they seem not to be able to get enough. I am not going to endorse any brands here, but if the deer won't touch what you have offered them, change it out for another brand. I have tried a brand from a mill in Texas that wild hogs will not even eat. This company usually has great corn, but the protein proved useless. So don't fill to capacity the first time, check to see if your herd will accept the feed you are trying.

As far as pellets go, there are a lot of private label pellets made all over. Local mills vary their mixtures. Some mixtures contain a little more corn that helps to get the deer started on the protein feed. You should always start your protein pellets off mixed with corn to help entice them to try it.

Starting the protein in the winter months and during tough conditions will help you get them to look for it every day. After they are established on the protein feed keep it out there for them year round for the best results. They will usually eat very little of it when their natural forage is plentiful, but it will be there when they need it.

You should also have good quality mineral blocks available at all times.

Supplemental feeding can be accomplished by different means. The method you choose to use in your presentation of the feed to the whitetail can vary depending on available cash and personal choices.

An inexpensive method is a typical feeder barrel with a free choice attachment bolted to it. Another method is the trough style protein feeders that are available. Still, another method that is more costly but touted to save feed is the timed protein feeders recently introduced by a couple of manufacturers.

These electronic feeders deliver protein pellets when you designate, at the quantity levels you determine. This helps you to feed fewer varmints, but by no means is this method more productive than free choice feeders. In my experience of always buying the latest and greatest, I find that the electronic protein feeders clog up often in wet conditions.

The bottom line on protein feed is, if you can afford it, do it. Any added level of supplemental feed will help, it does not have to be on an enormous scale to be somewhat effective. Supplemental feed will help you to have better deer year to year, even with variations in the natural habitat conditions.

Conversely, if you do not choose to use protein feeding in your regimen, don't worry. By following all of the other tenants of ADM, you will still produce the best trophy bucks your property has to offer, and that is the ultimate, achievable goal.

Don't let money discourage you. Go for it! You have everything to gain and nothing to lose. If you are going to have a lease, as most of us are, then go for the gold, stick to the plan, and the gold won't be far.

Section Summary
Let's look back

There are many types of protein feeds available. Many of them are merely rodent and varmint attractants.

Protein pellets also are not all equal. Some feeds will not be accepted by the deer; so, try different brands until you find the one that they prefer.

Aggressive Deer Management
The Fast Track to Trophy Bucks

Field notes

Food Plots

This topic is great, as a hunter can implement the ADM plan without any plot whatsoever. However, for the best results, adding quality nutritious forage to your herd's diet will increase the yield. There is no reason to suggest which mix you should plant, as you can find out what grows best in your area locally.

Match the crop with the available planting method at your disposal. Many times a property owner will plant for you with a little help, and all the seed provided.

There are also many implements that can be dragged behind an ATV, or even a truck, for light work in soil; or, your hunting group can pool their money together and buy a used tractor. With this you can plant and maintain your shooting lanes and lease roads.

Some plots can be used merely to entice the deer into the open, but you should try to stick with the best nutritional yield, for deciding on what to plant for the herd.

*Aggressive Deer Management
The Fast Track to Trophy Bucks*

Many "trophy" mixes are on the market and work pretty well. When picking a crop, check into drought tolerance as well as cold weather resistance. Whitetails love fresh, green chutes in the winter, when all else is dormant. The crops you plant this year, will not only help the herd this year, but will also be a factor on next years antler development, as the bucks will have nourishment after the rut to help them recover.

There are huge varieties of plants to choose from. Some seeds can simply be broadcast and still show favorable results, while others should be covered with earth for best results.

A good method of feeding and attracting deer is to plant a food plot of high quality forage. Then spread a broadcastable mix everywhere that is convenient for you to deliver it, such as your lease roads, and shooting lanes and any open areas conducive to growth. The rewards will be worth the toil.

Section Summary
Let's look back

Food plots are a very effective way to provide nutrition as well as a source of attraction. The methods for planting are varied from ATV's to tractors to hand broadcasters. The seeds are available as premixed feeds and individual seed variations. You can find plants that will grow in your area at local feed stores, just make sure you ask questions about the feed and make sure it is for planting in your region.

Zacch Smith

Field notes

Water Availability

The natural water supply on your property is a consideration that should be taken into account.

Whitetail deer are very prolific and traveling a few miles is no impediment to a deer, so water in the vicinity is all that is necessary. The more water the better, as the deer you seek may be able to stay closer in to where you may prefer him to be, this will help him avoid passing through the paths of other hunters.

If you hunt an area with cactus then deer will have a great source of water readily available.

If you hunt an area with very little water for deer, then I would suggest a water station that I have used in the past. It was very successful and definitely attracted deer; the deer even fought over the drinking rights.

The device should be blended into the surrounding habitat by camouflage paint and purposeful placement against trees or in brush to help it blend. Place the device in a feeder pen if livestock are present.

The watering device can be put together with a small trough, a barrel (plastic or metal), a small amount of water hose, a hose bib (off on valve) and a cheap float valve that can be obtained from feed stores.

The trough area should be relatively small to prevent animals from bathing in it and wasting the water, as well as to help keep the evaporation level low.

As far as filling the holding container, it is easily accomplished by using one of the 250 to 450 gallon water containers that fit in the back of a truck. Containers can be purchased at most larger feed stores and ranch supply stores. Filling it is easy, water is heavy and its height in the back of a truck lends it to be great for gravity fill. You may be surprised at the water pressure you have just from the weight of the water propelling it through the hose.

I am including a material list for you and instructions for the basic unit. you can vary the shape and other factors to make it work for you.

Material list- 1- barrel, 1-4' length of water hose, 1- on/off valve, 1- float valve, 1-3 to 5 gallon trough,1- hose coupler from barrel and 4-8"x16" blocks.

The blocks are used for elevation, the barrel will sit on the blocks to insure gravity flow. Connect the hose to the on/off valve that you will have connected to a low point on the barrel. Now you can run the hose to the float valve that you have fastened to the small trough. At this point you can fill it with water and the device will operate until all of the water is consumed.

Section Summary
Let's look back

Traveling a few miles for water is no big feat for deer, so you don't have to have water all over the property. Water availability helps to keep your herd in close and keeps them from having to move very far for water.

If you are very remote from water, then you can supplement the water supply and draw in deer. I tried it and it works.

Zacch Smith

Field notes

Chapter VI

Our ADM Goal

To exact calculations, educated guesses and common sense. To science, theories and awe inspiring creation.

Zacch Smith

What Scores can you Expect From Free Ranging Bucks?

Boone and Crocket scores and Pope and Young scores are the basis of measurement for all of our goals. These forms of trophy validation are useful as a means to talk about and reference quality and size, in understandable and relatable terms.

Let me state that there are thousands of great looking, outstanding and very impressive trophies that do not score very high on an inch scale; but, they score great on visual appeal and most certainly are still trophies. Visually appealing bucks that make it on our wall, without having big scores, are wonderful and respected; however, inches are where the ink hits the paper.

Free ranging bucks can achieve enormous proportions, especially when they are supplemented with feed. But on average an old buck doesn't necessarily equate to a big buck.

Here is a break down of approximately what to expect, as far as a Boone & Crocket (B&C) scores in an average herd with average genetics and good forage.

The approximate overall B&C average of unmanaged bucks that reach maturity is in the 130 class range. Lesser bucks are as common as bucks that are slightly larger.

When we are searching for bucks that are much larger, we come to the realization that they are few in number, but they most certainly do exist. As we hunt, we get the chance to prove it every so often even on unmanaged land.

Here, is an approximate age, and score break down. You can expect to see scores like this in an average unmanaged herd scenario. Due to the differing genetic variables in herds you should adjust this information up or down to approximate the region or area you are hunting.

- 1 and 2-year old bucks vary dramatically but are not worth mentioning.
- 3-year old bucks are usually from 115 to 125 B&C points.

- 4-year old bucks are usually from 120 to 135 B&C points.
- 5-year old bucks are usually from 125 to 145 B&C points.
- 6-year old bucks are usually from 135 to 160 B&C points.

During good range conditions, if you find that you have bucks that fall well below the score levels indicated here and the buck is in the upper end age group, then you have a cull in front of you and he should be harvested.

Five and six-year old bucks that fall into the low 120 class have no place in a managed herd during good range conditions.

Looking at what we have to expect, we turn to Aggressive Deer Management to increase the average buck antler score and produce more trophy bucks than would ever be the case without management.

Section Summary
Let's look back

Free ranging bucks will usually reach average levels of antler size, with superior bucks being the exception. We looked at the average antler score you can expect from free ranging herds. What we found is that bucks should be directed to produce the results we want, so we then turn our eyes to Aggressive Deer Management to up the ante.

Aggressive Deer Management
The Fast Track to Trophy Bucks

Field notes

Zacch Smith

ADM
What We Wish to Accomplish By Administering This Technique

In the previous pages we discussed what we could expect on average land with average genetics and average habitat.

We are not hunting for average bucks. ADM is not about harvesting average bucks; it is about harvesting outstanding bucks.

Aggressive deer management is the fastest way to achieve our goal. We will not wait around for a fluke that brings us a chance at a trophy. No, we are taking control of the outcome and changing the average antler size of the bucks on our property. We are altering the genetically imposed limits that are now present on our property.

We will boldly harvest unwanted bucks that we do not wish to have breed and control the numbers for population as well as for ratio. In so doing, we will redirect the antler characteristics of our herd.

By being deliberate in our selection of which bucks to leave in the herd, we will see the traits of those bucks contribute to advance the antler development and we will witness the undesirable traits diminish.

By harvesting the excess does and cull bucks as per plan, we will alter the genetic direction on the first attempt.

When we adhere to the plan, it means you should harvest them at the correct time. You can't wait until you feel like removing excess deer. You must act fast. Be aggressive with the management. Set up rules and follow them, assign hunters to remove their does on opening weekend.

If you spot cull bucks that should go, there will be no better time to remove them than that very moment when you determine the buck is a cull.

If you are going to start supplemental feeding then pack up next weekend and go start it. Don't just talk about what you plan to do; planning doesn't produce the big boys like action does.

Section Summary
Let's look back

Aggressive Deer Management is the path we are going to take to alter the average size of the mature bucks we wish to harvest. This is the fastest method possible, but it won't work if you don't implement it. Make sure everyone in your group is involved and is part of the program. Motivation will grow and success will be inevitable.

*Aggressive Deer Management
The Fast Track to Trophy Bucks*

Field notes

Zacch Smith

Chapter VII

Salient Synopsis For Instant Field Deployment

To hunting, hunters, and the hunted.

I salute you.

Zacch Smith

Quick Guide To Management

If you have made it this far then you know the reasons behind the direction and you know the variables that may apply.

Let this serve, along with common sense to be a general referral tool in your day-to-day management.

Step 1

If you are going to start supplemental feeding then do it now. You should have started before you read this far in the book.

Step 2

If you have hunted this property before write down your impressions of the habitat from last year and your thoughts on the deer population.

- Observe your range condition.
- Are you in a drought?
- Is the habitat abundant with plenty of forage for the whitetail?

Step 3

Follow the directions in the section on deer census to do your census.

Write down the results.

Step 4

Combining all of your previous knowledge of the property, if any, with the evidence you find as to the condition of the habitat, you are now ready to decide if your population is too high, or to low, or is it just about right. Talk to the other hunters on the property and get a consensus.

Combining common sense with your census will provide you with usable numbers that are not unlike number you would receive from a paid helicopter census. Many times because of familiarity with your hunting property you are better qualified to make the judgments then you may realize.

Step 5

Here is where the plan comes together, but first this advice. You are about to start hunting and now is as good a time as ever to get all hunters involved to commit to not taking any good mature breeding bucks until after the rut takes place! This is the best way to get a jumpstart and be aggressive. You will have removed the culls and trimmed down the ratio so let's make sure our best bucks get to breed all the does this year. If I can pass them up, then so can you! Now let's roll on.

You have by now recorded your best estimate as to your ratio and population so the next step is to implement the ratio and population adjustment phase. If you hunt with a group, then assign the number of does that must be removed to each of the hunters proportionally. Make everyone aware of which bucks will be considered cull bucks and lay down the strategy for taking them out of circulation. I am sure I do not need to remind you when to remove these unneeded deer.

Step 6

Initiate the ratio and cull portion of the plan on opening day. Keep in contact with everyone by radio if feasible while performing the culling of bucks. This will help greatly, as discussing the attributes of individual bucks with other knowledgeable hunters can be of great help in the determination of culls. If a buck is determined a cull, don't let him walk another step!

Step 7

Carefully observe your herd and get input from each hunter. Does it look like you called it right, do you need to make any adjustment to your initial thoughts on the numbers? Keep track of the age structure of your deer, the buck to doe ratio, etc. After the first weekend you have already set the stage for healthier deer. Through the culling of the inferior bucks, you are guaranteeing that only the better bucks you are allowing to remain in the herd, will breed this year.

There is already more browse for your bucks as you have eliminated the extra does and cull bucks that were previously using up key nutrients.

Step 8

Keep taking notes and adjust as needed; your off and running, just repeat the process. You can continue the trophy buck policy of waiting until after the rut for another year or not, it's up to you. If you believe a few mature deer have the exact traits you must have, then you may let them get though rut again if you desire.

This is not mandatory as you are now eliminating the culls early enough that they will play no role in breeding, ever. As long as you keep this up, the herd will respond favorably.

Order of operation

1. Start supplemental feed
2. Observe the herd and the habitat
3. If known, write down information you know from last year that can be useful for this year: like habitat condition, ratio, or population estimates, if any
4. Census
5. Harvest plan
6. Ratio and cull harvest implementation
7. Observation, adjustments if warranted
8. Lather, rinse, repeat

Zacch Smith

Population Age Structure

While taking your census you will be noting the age structure of the deer. You should label them as you see them to the best of your ability.

When the spotters call out what they see, they should specify: fawn, yearling, two-year old, three-year old, four-year old, etc.

The spotters should be familiar with discerning the information you will need, to take that position on your census team. Determining age during a census is difficult, so you will be approximating the age class of the deer.

To gain a more precise age group break down, you will need to have your hunting group sit out in stands and carefully observe, take notes and preferably video the deer they see. Now you can put all the information together and derive a pretty close number as to how many deer in each age group exist on your land. The age groups should be adjusted thru harvesting and would ideally look like this. A 25% percent adult buck population, with bucks aged 0-1.5 years old also at 25% and the 2.5-4.5 year olds at 50% is a good point to be at and you can make that happen by culling or letting bucks walk, depending on if you are high or low.

I have included forms in the back of the book so you will have a place that you can plug in the age class separation numbers and this information will help you each year to see how the population changes, so you can make adjustments as needed. The age classification information is more important for the buck population as you are managing for buck quality and quantity. The does' age structure is usually varied. The information you record about the age classes of the bucks will be used to make sure you have a good number of bucks maturing to harvest age each year.

Management Comparison

As a casual observer of management plans implemented by hunters, as well as property owners, I find that in many cases the plan is unclear. The objectives are only implied not defined. The actions taken to implement the plans are reactionary, delayed and most of the time not culminated by the conclusion of the season.

Obviously this does not work and in many cases the whole thing becomes discouraging and gets out of hand. Our intention is to be proactive: take control of the outcome of your trophy hunting future by implementing Aggressive Deer Management. Set the standards, assign the numbers, and get the momentum rolling before deer season so on opening day you will be eager to go. Immediately, start harvesting the excess does in your herd as well as every cull buck you spot. If you bow hunt, then that's even better. Remove the deer that must be eliminated for ratio equalizing and population control as well as culls, as quickly as you can.

The only time you should ever use a late doe season for removing does is if at the last minute you realize that you still have too many does in your herd.

Harvesting does and culls early and fast, is the only logical way if you want the rest of the herd to be able to utilize <u>every</u> available resource. Every day that you wait to harvest the culls and the does that you eventually plan on getting around to harvesting, they are depleting the resources that should be left for the stock you are trying to improve.

Waiting leads to procrastination and procrastination leads to complacency and this is why many management goals are never achieved.

Aggressive Deer Management is a plan designed to be straight forward, defined, logical, easy to implement, goal-oriented; and because of its aggressive implementation, you will avoid problems that are common with average plans.

Your ratio will be corrected on your first hunting weekend; culls are removed every time one presents itself. This results in most of the work being accomplished on the first week of hunting season and lends the rest of the season for fun and observation, as well as serious trophy hunting.

No more stress over whether or not the culls and does will be taken this year, because by the first weekend you are substantially complete.

Now with your ratio starting off adjusted, as it should be, only your best bucks will breed. The younger bucks due to the ratio and lack of dominance will remain subordinate non-breeders until they reach maturity or show themselves to be culls and you remove them from the herd.

This reduces stress and guides your genetic direction as planned. Aggressive ratio adjustment also eliminates the anxiety of harvesting the does after the rut, at a time when you can't tell if you are harvesting the does bred by your best bucks, which would defeat your purpose.

Many property owners may need these tenets explained to them so they will allow lessees to manage the deer. You may need to go over everything in detail to get them on board or give them a copy of ADM, so they can be in control and represent a leadership position in the endeavor.

The owners will benefit just as much as the hunters, knowing that the hunters are good stewards of the land and that management is an on going proposition that will last for years; not to mention that the deer quality will go up.

If you have an unusually skeptical owner who imposes buck and doe limits on you that do nothing for management, then he or she does not fully understand what is needed to manage the herd and develop the trophy class of bucks you desire. The trophy class bucks are the very reason you are paying for the privilege to hunt.

When this is the case, humbly give him a copy of ADM and respectfully discuss management with them to generate the dialogue conducive to the goals of both the hunters and the property owners.

Synopsis

What I hope we have accomplished is an understanding of Aggressive Deer Management.

Using your own common since combined with your previous and future field experience and this book, you can feel eager to reap the rewards.

By taking a broad look at the scope of management before us, we see the big picture. In order to harvest mature trophy bucks we must consider what it takes to make a mature trophy buck. It takes nutrition, genetics and age.

Therefore, we improve nutrition by keeping the population well within capacity limits so as to eliminate the chance that the competition for food will adversely affect the population.

We supplement food available if we can by planting or broadcasting nutritious forage plants, feeding protein and mineral offerings.

We direct the genetic makeup of the herd by selectively removing undesirable bucks from the herd before they ever have a chance to breed, carefully taking into consideration every aspect of determining a cull buck.

We are to be relentless in the aggressive disposition of cull bucks.

Determining a cull buck is to be done with the utmost care taking into account the habitat condition and it's affect on the current crop of bucks. The age of the buck tempered with your assessment of the other bucks that are in the same size and age group will provide the answer to whether or not he is a cull.

With this information in hand, you can confidently determine which bucks to cull. Undue stress over cull determination should be avoided. A mistake made while culling bucks will not have a long-term detrimental effect.

Finally, another huge factor is age. A buck does not reach his full potential until his fifth and sixth-year of life. A buck must be allowed to finish growing his skeletal system before we can expect him to produce his best set of antlers.

Sadly, in many cases hunters have never had the opportunity to actually see a five or six-year old buck because of the reverse management phenomenon prevalent in some areas. Let the bucks with potential reach five and six-years of age and the chance to harvest a trophy will present itself.

Reflections

Now that you have read the book, the onus is on you. What are you going to do about managing your herd? You have the tools to make your decisions. You know how to improve your herd and grow the bucks in it, to their fullest potential.

Here is what we have learned. In order for our herd to produce the best bucks that it is capable of producing, our guidance is needed. We assess the habitat conditions and make a judgment call as to the deer population versus the available food supply.

Using one of the methods outlined in the previous chapters, you take a count to be able to make an educated guess as to the population numbers and the age/sex breakdown. You may by virtue of your intimate knowledge of your herd, be able to determine what is needed for population control and then make adjustments in the population through harvesting any excess deer from the herd.

The population control is performed in harmony with ratio control. After cutting the population numbers down, we should also be at the correct ratio.

Timing is crucial to the fast deployment and quick success of the plan. The population adjustment should be made at the start of the season: the faster and earlier the better. Culls should be taken at this time and any culls that you see during the season should also be harvested at the very moment you identify them as a cull, never let them remain in the herd. You do not have to harvest the does from your most prized hunting spot, be creative set up and harvest them anywhere that you prefer.

Aggressive Deer Management is exactly that and to perform the technique in a less than aggressive manner will slow the effects. Population control and ratio control as well as culling inferior bucks must be done at the earliest possible time. When you are culling bucks, keep in mind that you will be culling some young bucks each year in order to keep the ratio correct and maintain overall population numbers each year. The young bucks you choose to cull will be the deer in that age category with the least evident potential as compared to the same age class of bucks.

Once you have the population at the correct level, you will need to remove as many deer each year as are added though reproduction. You will be removing the bucks in every age class as necessary. The bucks with the least potential for growing trophy quality antlers will be culled.

Supplemental feeding is a great way to enhance the antler development. Protein feeders as well as food plots are recommended although not absolutely necessary. Huge trophy bucks are produced from ranches that just manage for quality and do not go all out on supplemental feed; however, the deer produced would surely be even bigger if they added a good nutrition program.

If you are trying to get off to a roaring start then consider not taking any mature trophy bucks on the first year of implementation until after the rut, to make sure that the best bucks you have in your herd were able to breed the does.

By directing your herd through Aggressive Deer Management, you will be avoiding most of the common problems associated with the average reactionary based plans. You will correct the population and ratio numbers before the critical time periods of rut and winter occurs, thus enhancing the effects tremendously. Deer that should be culled are culled early leaving all of the forage they would consume for the remaining deer. The ratio is adjusted before the rut, which encourages the proper preferred bucks to be the only breeding bucks available.

When you correct the ratio and population numbers at the end of the season, as most hunters do, then you are doing things in reverse order. The corrections to the ratio must be made before the rut. The rut is the reason for the numbers to be adjusted in the first place, so does it make any logical since to adjust them post rut? I cannot see any benefit in waiting, so why do people manage this way? It's probably because no one every explained the reasoning to them before.

When deciding on which does to take, I will recommend harvesting the old doe that always snorts and alarms the entire herd of your existence. An old doe that is hunter wise will often eliminate chances at mature bucks by indicating your presence. So when you cull does, harvest the does with that ability and the less experienced does will lead the bucks right to you during the rut. The weary does will often avoid your area altogether and lead bucks away during the rut.

Another factor to consider is that the old does will be of the genetic pool before you started managing. The young does will be the offspring from your chosen bucks. So for the first three years, eliminating a good number of the older does will actually enhance your program by insuring that the up coming does, as well as the bucks, are from the genetic lines you are directing. The older does are better breeders, so when the new crop of does reach maturity you will want keep a few more in the older age class for breeding.

Following the plan as outlined will produce the fastest possible results and implementing the plan is as easy as going hunting. Just review how to determine a cull buck, share the information with the other managers and hunters in your group and contact your hunting neighbors to get them involved.

Talking with the hunters, the owners or the managers of your surrounding properties is a key element to long-term success and continuing improvement, as well as the fact that it is very gratifying to know that you may have helped set the tone for the whole area you are hunting. Keep in mind that the genetic pool around you can also work to everyone's benefit if you encourage others to join in.

Earlier I asked the question: what are you going to do about managing your herd? Well, I believe I already know the answer. So let's get aggressive and grow some trophy bucks, plan it out, put it on paper and start on opening day. Good luck and good hunting.

Aggressive Deer Management
The Fast Track to Trophy Bucks

Worksheets

Percentage forms

Census forms

Hunter responsibility forms

Buck harvest forms

Zacch Smith

ADM Chart	Age	Percentage	Actual Number	Actual % of Herd
0-1 year old bucks				
2-year old bucks				
3-year old bucks				
4-year old bucks				
5-years old and above				

*Aggressive Deer Management
The Fast Track to Trophy Bucks*

ADM Chart	Age	Percentage	Actual Number	Actual % of Herd
0-1 year old bucks				
2-year old bucks				
3-year old bucks				
4-year old bucks				
5-years old and above				

ADM

EASY CENSUS FORM
Step 1

CENSUS METHOD USED
Line method
Spot light method

Square footage figures

Line or road segment parameters

	Segment length	Segment width	Total area
_____		X	
_____		X	
_____		X	
_____		X	
_____		X	
_____		X	
_____		X	
_____		X	
_____		X	
_____		X	
_____		X	
_____		X	
_____		X	
_____		X	
_____		X	
_____		X	
_____		X	
_____		X	

Total square footage observed   _____

Above square footage divided by   43,560'

This number is the total acreage observed   _____

Aggressive Deer Management
The Fast Track to Trophy Bucks

ADM
EASY CENSUS FORM
Step 2

Total quantity of deer observed

Total number of bucks observed

Total number of doe's observed

Total number of young antlerless deer

Take the total number of young antlerless deer and divide it by 2, then add that number to the buck deer number and the doe deer number for your Adjusted total number of bucks and does

Adjusted Buck number

Adjusted Doe number

Total number of deer inhabiting property

Now take the total number of acres

And divide by the total number of deer

This is your deer per acre number

171

Zacch Smith

ADM

EASY CENSUS FORM
Step 1

CENSUS METHOD USED
Line method
Spot light method

Square footage figures

Line or road segment parameters

	Segment length	Segment width	Total area
_____	X		
_____	X		
_____	X		
_____	X		
_____	X		
_____	X		
_____	X		
_____	X		
_____	X		
_____	X		
_____	X		
_____	X		
_____	X		
_____	X		
_____	X		
_____	X		
_____	X		
_____	X		

Total square footage observed   [   ]

Above square footage divided by   [43,560']

This number is the total acreage observed   [   ]

Aggressive Deer Management
The Fast Track to Trophy Bucks

ADM
EASY CENSUS FORM
Step 2

Total quantity of deer observed

Total number of bucks observed

Total number of doe's observed

Total number of young antlerless deer

Take the total number of young antlerless deer and divide it by 2, then add that number to the buck deer number and the doe deer number for your adjusted total number of bucks and does

Adjusted Buck number

Adjusted Doe number

Total number of deer inhabiting property

Now take the total number of acres

And divide by the total number of deer

This is your deer per acre number

Zacch Smith

ADM

EASY CENSUS FORM
Step 1

CENSUS METHOD USED
Line method
Spot light method

Square footage figures

Line or road segment parameters

	Segment length	Segment width	Total area
_____	X		
_____	X		
_____	X		
_____	X		
_____	X		
_____	X		
_____	X		
_____	X		
_____	X		
_____	X		
_____	X		
_____	X		
_____	X		
_____	X		
_____	X		
_____	X		
_____	X		
_____	X		

Total square footage observed [ ]

Above square footage divided by [43,560']

This number is the total acreage observed [ ]

Aggressive Deer Management
The Fast Track to Trophy Bucks

ADM
EASY CENSUS FORM
Step 2

Total quantity of deer observed ☐

Total number of bucks observed ☐

Total number of doe's observed ☐

Total number of young antlerless deer ☐

Take the total number of young antlerless deer and divide it by 2, then add that number to the buck deer number and the doe deer number for your adjusted total number of bucks and does

Adjusted Buck number ☐

Adjusted Doe number ☐

Total number of deer inhabiting property ☐

Now take the total number of acres ☐

And divide by the total number of deer ☐

This is your deer per acre number ☐

Zacch Smith

	EASY CENSUS
ADM	**FORM**
	Step 1

CENSUS METHOD USED
Line method
Spot light method

Square footage figures

Line or road segment parameters

Segment length	Segment width	Total area
X		
X		
X		
X		
X		
X		
X		
X		
X		
X		
X		
X		
X		
X		
X		
X		
X		
X		

Total square footage observed

Above square footage divided by   43,560'

This number is the total acreage observed

Aggressive Deer Management
The Fast Track to Trophy Bucks

ADM
EASY CENSUS FORM
Step 2

Total quantity of deer observed

Total number of bucks observed

Total number of doe's observed

Total number of young antlerless deer

Take the total number of young antlerless deer and divide it by 2, then add that number to the buck deer number and the doe deer number for your adjusted total number of bucks and does

Adjusted Buck number

Adjusted Doe number

Total number of deer inhabiting property

Now take the total number of acres

And divide by the total number of deer

This is your deer per acre number

177

Zacch Smith

	EASY CENSUS
ADM	FORM
	Step 1

CENSUS METHOD USED
Line method
Spot light method   Square footage figures

Line or road segment parameters

	Segment length	Segment width	Total area
_____	X		
_____	X		
_____	X		
_____	X		
_____	X		
_____	X		
_____	X		
_____	X		
_____	X		
_____	X		
_____	X		
_____	X		
_____	X		
_____	X		
_____	X		
_____	X		
_____	X		
_____	X		

Total square footage observed   [   ]

Above square footage divided by   [43,560']

This number is the total acreage observed   [   ]

Aggressive Deer Management
The Fast Track to Trophy Bucks

ADM
EASY CENSUS FORM
Step 2

Total quantity of deer observed

Total number of bucks observed

Total number of doe's observed

Total number of young antlerless deer

Take the total number of young antlerless deer and divide it by 2, then add that number to the buck deer number and the doe deer number for your adjusted total number of bucks and does

Adjusted Buck number

Adjusted Doe number

Total number of deer inhabiting property

Now take the total number of acres

And divide by the total number of deer

This is your deer per acre number

179

Hunter Responsibility Chart

Hunters Name	Required Does	Required Bucks
Totals		

Aggressive Deer Management
The Fast Track to Trophy Bucks

Hunter Responsibility Chart

Hunters Name	Required Does	Required Bucks
Totals		

Zacch Smith

Hunter Responsibility Chart

Hunters Name	Required Does	Required Bucks
Totals		

Aggressive Deer Management
The Fast Track to Trophy Bucks

Hunter Responsibility Chart

Hunters Name	Required Does	Required Bucks
Totals		

Zacch Smith

Buck Harvest Chart

Hunters Initials & Area	Approx. Age	Weight	B&C Gross Score	Date Harvested	Time
Average all totals to help check progress each year					

Buck Harvest Chart

Hunters Initials & Area	Approx. Age	Weight	B&C Gross Score	Date Harvested	Time
Average all totals to help check progress each year					

Zacch Smith

Buck Harvest Chart

Hunters Initials & Area	Approx. Age	Weight	B&C Gross Score	Date Harvested	Time
Average all totals to help check progress each year					

Aggressive Deer Management
The Fast Track to Trophy Bucks

Buck Harvest Chart

Hunters Initials & Area	Approx. Age	Weight	B&C Gross Score	Date Harvested	Time
Average all totals to help check progress each year					

Zacch Smith

Yearly Summary Log

Date:

Age of Buck harvested	weight	Score 3-4yrs.	Score 4-5yrs.	Score 5-6+yrs.

Average or tally each of the above columns

Aggressive Deer Management
The Fast Track to Trophy Bucks

Yearly Summary Log

Date:

Age of Buck harvested	weight	Score 3-4yrs.	Score 4-5yrs.	Score 5-6+yrs.

Average or tally each of the above columns

Zacch Smith

Yearly Summary Log

Date:

Age of Buck harvested	weight	Score 3-4yrs.	Score 4-5yrs.	Score 5-6+yrs.

Average or tally each of the above columns

Aggressive Deer Management

Visit

www.AggressiveDeerManagement.com

Hunting information and links to other sites

Book purchase information and discount shipping price for orders thru this direct sales location.

All major credit cards accepted as well as most other forms of payment.

Book cost is $34.00 + shipping.

Orders can be mailed to:

Aggressive Deer Management

8425 Old Hwy. 81

Temple, Texas 76501

About the Author

Zacch Smith is a patriot and a lifetime member of the N.R.A. as well as an avid hunter and student of the whitetail deer. He has spent many years hunting whitetails and now for the last few years he has spent every available moment studying his quarry to discover the truths to the whitetail management questions that have been impeding management decisions for years.

With this simple guide he has filled the need for a plan that will produce results fast, his progressive approach will be the new standard for deer management anywhere that hunters or managers seek dramatic quick trophy development. The aggressive technique he describes will produce the fastest possible results for anyone who implements it.

Printed in the United States
20493LVS00005B/283-363